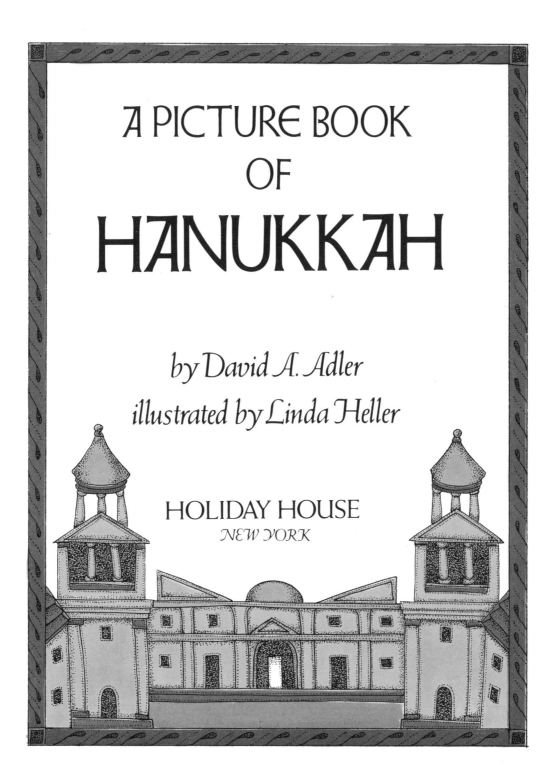

A PICTURE BOOK OF HANUKKAH

by David A. Adler

illustrated by Linda Heller

HOLIDAY HOUSE
NEW YORK

Library of Congress Cataloging in Publication Data

Adler, David A.
A picture book of Hanukkah.

Summary: Discusses how the celebration of Hanukkah
came about, what it signifies, and ways in which it is
celebrated today.

1. Hanukkah—Juvenile literature. [1. Hanukkah]
I. Heller, Linda, ill. II. Title.
BM695.H3A653   296.4′35   82-2942
ISBN 0-8234-0458-7   AACR2

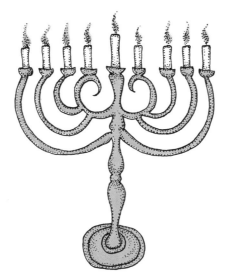

To Uncle Arno and Aunt Edith

D. A. A.

To Ann

L. H.

The Story of Hanukkah

The story of Hanukkah begins in Israel long ago. The country was called Judea then, and the Jews who lived there did not rule their land. Different kings with their armies marched through Judea. First one ruled the land, then another. But while Judea was ruled by different kings, the Jews lived there as they always had. The farmers planted and harvested. The shepherds watched their sheep. And on holidays they all went up to the Temple in Jerusalem.

The Temple was beautiful. It stood on top of a mountain. Inside were gold crowns and gates covered with gold and silver. There was a *ner tamid*, a light that always burned, and a gold vine with gold leaves and grapes hanging from it. No iron was used in building the Temple. That's because iron is a tool of war, and the Temple was a place of peace. It was called "The House of God."

There were no idols in the Temple. Other people worshipped many gods. They prayed and bowed to idols. But the Jews, led by the high priest, prayed to just one god, the God who created the heaven and earth.

The Jews kept their holidays. They lived in peace until a Greek, Antiochus the Fourth, ruled Judea.

It was not enough for Antiochus that his people paid him high taxes. He wanted them all to take Greek names, read Greek books, and play Greek sports.

Antiochus forced the Jews to take a new high priest. The priest's name was Menelaus. Soon after Menelaus was made high priest, he began stealing gold and silver from the Temple and sending it to Antiochus.

The Jews hated the new high priest. While Antiochus was fighting a war in Egypt, a small army of Jewish soldiers surrounded the Temple. They forced Menelaus out.

But then Antiochus returned. His army was with him. He saw the soldiers in Jerusalem and thought the Jews were rising up against him. With his army, he stormed the city. They tore down the city walls. It was the Sabbath. The Jews wouldn't fight back and thousands were killed. Homes were burned. Women and children were carried off and sold as slaves.

Antiochus and his men marched into the Temple. They marched out with everything that he and his men could carry. Later a Greek idol was placed in the Temple. Any Jew who refused to bow and sacrifice an animal to the idol was killed. So were Jews who lit Sabbath candles or studied Jewish law.

The king's soldiers went throughout Judea and forced the Jews to bow and worship Greek idols. Some Jews obeyed the king. Many others didn't and were killed.

Then the king's men came to the town of Modin. They set up their idol and asked an old priest named Mattathias to worship it. Mattathias refused. But another man was frightened and was ready to worship the idol. Mattathias rushed forward. He struck the man and one of the soldiers. He threw down the idol and called out, "Whoever is for the Lord, our God, follow me!" And he ran off into the hills. His five sons and many other Jews followed him.

Antiochus heard what happened in Modin. He sent
an army after Mattathias and his followers. But each time
the soldiers came near, the rocks and caves seemed to open
up. Brave Jews attacked the strong army of Antiochus.
Then they ran back to the hills and hid.

One army general remembered that the Jews would
not fight on the Sabbath, so that's when he attacked.
Many Jews were killed until Mattathias told his men that
they must fight back, even on the Sabbath.

The Jews were farmers and shepherds. But they fought like brave soldiers. First they fought under Mattathias. Then, when Mattathias died, his son Judah became their leader. Judah was called the Maccabee, the hammer. The people who fought with him were called Maccabees.

Antiochus sent his best generals with large armies to fight the Maccabees. The armies came with bows, arrows, swords, horses, and armored elephants. For one battle, slave traders even came along leading empty wagons. After the battle, the traders planned to capture the beaten, frightened Maccabees and sell them as slaves.

It never happened.

The Maccabees surprised the armies of Antiochus. Once the Maccabees caught them in a narrow pass between two mountains. From the tops and sides of the mountains, it was easy for the Maccabees to fight their enemies down below.

Another time, Judah knew that the soldiers of Antiochus were ready to attack. He lit a ring of campfires and
led his men away. Then, while half the enemy's army was
attacking the empty campsite, Judah and the Maccabees
surprised the other half.

In the final battle, there were more than six of the enemy for each Maccabee. But still, the mighty army of Antiochus was beaten. And Judah led the Maccabees to Jerusalem.

The Temple in Jerusalem was overgrown with thorns and weeds. It was filled with garbage. When the Maccabees first saw it, they cried. They tore their clothes and mourned. Then they worked to clean the Temple. They built a new altar, new gates, and new doors.

When the time came to light the *ner tamid*, the Maccabees searched for oil. They found just one small jar, enough to burn for just one day. But the oil in that small jar burned and burned until more oil could be prepared. The oil which was enough for one day burned for eight days, and the *ner tamid*, the light that always burned, did not go out.

On the twenty-fifth day of the Hebrew month of Kislev, the Temple became again the "House of God." The Jews celebrated. They prayed and sang for eight days. Then Judah declared that every year, on the twenty-fifth of Kislev, an eight-day holiday would begin. The holiday was called Hanukkah which means dedication. It celebrates the day the Temple was rededicated to God.

That was over two thousand years ago. But today, all over the world, Jews still celebrate Hanukkah.

The Holiday of Hanukkah

We light candles in our homes on each of the eight nights of Hanukkah. And, as the candles burn, we sing about the Hanukkah miracles.

We eat *latkes*, potato pancakes fried in oil. And we play a game with a square spinning top, a *dreidel*. On each of the four sides of the *dreidel* is a different Hebrew letter. They are the first four letters of the Hebrew sentence, *nes gadol hayah sham*, which means, "A great miracle happened there."

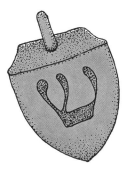

In many homes children are given gifts and Hanukkah *gelt*. Hanukkah *gelt* is Hanukkah money, and it is often used in the *dreidel* games. The gifts are just an added way to make the holiday a happy one.

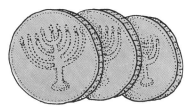

The candles, the songs, the oil in the *latkes,* and the letters on the *dreidel* remind us of the miracles that happened during the time of Judah and his father Mattathias. The miracles, of course, are the small jar of oil that burned for so long and the small group of Maccabees who fought a mighty king and won.

Ever since that first Hanukkah, Jews just like the Maccabees have fought for the right to pray to God and live as Jews. And today, in certain parts of the world, Jews are still fighting for the very same things.